AMERICAN X-VEHICLES

An Inventory—X-1 to X-50

Centennial of Flight Edition

by Dennis R. Jenkins, Tony Landis, and Jay Miller

Monographs in Aerospace History No. 31

SP-2003-4531

June 2003

Suggested Further Reading

At the Edge of Space: The X-15 Flight Program, by Milton O. Thompson, Smithsonian Institution Press, 1992.
Hypersonic: The Story of the North American X-15, by Dennis R. Jenkins and Tony R. Landis, Specialty Press, 2003.
The X-Planes: X-1 to X-45, by Jay Miller, Midland Counties Publishing, 2001.
Always Another Dawn: The Story of a Rocket Test Pilot, by Scott Crossfield, The World Publishing Company, 1960
(reprinted by Arno Press in 1971 and again by Ayer Company Publishers in 1999).
Hypersonics Before the Shuttle: A Concise History of the X-15, by Dennis R. Jenkins, SP-2000-4518, NASA, 2000.
Toward Mach 2: The Douglas D-558 Program, edited by J. D. Hunley, SP-4222, NASA, 1999.
Flying Without Wings: NASA Lifting Bodies and the Birth of the Space Shuttle, by Milton O. Thompson and Curtis
Peebles, Smithsonian Institution Press, 1999.

Front Cover Photo

*A group picture of Douglas airplanes, taken for a photographic promotion in 1954 at what is now known as the Dryden Flight Research
Center at Edwards Air Force Base, California. The photo includes the X-3 (in front, Air Force serial number 49-2892) then clockwise
D-558-I, XF4D-1 (a Navy jet fighter prototype not flown by the NACA), and the first D-558-II (NACA tail number 143, Navy
bureau number 37973), which was flown only once by the NACA. (NASA photo E-1239)*

Library of Congress Cataloging-in-Publication Data

Jenkins, Dennis R.
American X-vehicles: an inventory, X-1 to X-50/by Dennis R. Jenkins, Tony Landis, and Jay Miller.
p.cm.—(Monographs in aerospace history; no.) (NASA history series) (NASA SP-2003-4531)
Includes bibliographical references and index.
1. Research aircraft—United States—History. I. Landis, Tony. II. Miller, Jay, 1948-III.
Title. IV. Series. V. Series: NASA history series VI. NASA SP-4531.

TL567.R47J45 2003
629.133'0973—dc21

2003051364

National Aeronautics and Space Administration
NASA Office of External Relations
NASA History Office
Washington, DC 20546

Table of Contents

For a while, it seemed the series of experimental aircraft sponsored by the U. S. government had run its course. Between the late 1940s and the late 1970s, almost thirty designations had been allocated to aircraft meant to explore new flight regimes or untried technologies. Then, largely, it ended. But there was a resurgence in the mid- to late-1990s, and as we enter the fourth year of the new millennia, the designations are up to X-50.

Many have a misconception that X-vehicles have always explored the high-speed and high-altitude flight regimes—something popularized by Chuck Yeager in the original X-1 and the exploits of the twelve men that flew the X-15. Although these flight regimes have always been in the spotlight, many others have been explored by X-vehicles. The little Bensen X-25 never exceeded 85 mph, and others were limited to speeds of several hundred mph.

There has been some criticism that the use of X designations has been corrupted somewhat by including what are essentially prototypes of future operational aircraft, especially the two JSF demonstrators. But this is not new—the X-11 and X-12 from the 1950s were going to be prototypes of the Atlas intercontinental ballistic missile, and the still-born Lockheed X-27 was always intended as a prototype of a production aircraft. So although this practice does not represent the best use of "X" designations, it is not without precedent.

Jay Miller
Arlington, Texas

Dennis R. Jenkins
Cape Canaveral, Florida

Tony Landis
Lancaster, California

The experimental aircraft fleet at the Flight Research Center in 1957. Clockwise from left front: X-1A, D-558-I, XF-92A, X-5, D-558-II, X-4, and the X-3 in the center. (NASA photo E-2889)

Bell Aircraft Company

First Generation X-1

First Flight:	25 January 1946	**Sponsors:**	USAF
Last Flight:	23 October 1951	**Fastest Flight:**	Mach 1.45 (960 mph)
Total Flights:	157	**Highest Flight:**	69,000 feet

The second of the three first generation Bell X-1s. Chuck Yeager used the first X-1 to break the sound barrier on 14 October 1947.
(Bell Aircraft via the Jay Miller Collection)

Initially designated the XS-1, (the S, which stood for Supersonic, was dropped early in the program), the X-1 was the first aircraft given an "X" designation, and became the first aircraft to exceed the speed of sound in controlled level flight on 14 October 1947. On this flight, the first X-1 (nicknamed *Glamorous Glennis*) was piloted by Captain Charles E. "Chuck" Yeager, who achieved 700 mph (Mach 1.06) at approximately 45,000 feet.

Beginning a precedent that survives to this day, the X-1 was air-launched—in this case carried under a Boeing B-29 Superfortress to an altitude of approximately 20,000 feet. The X-1 program was extremely productive, proving much of the technology necessary to produce the first-generation of supersonic combat aircraft. Many structural and aero-dynamic advances were pioneered by the first generation X-1s, including extremely thin yet exceptionally strong wing sections, supersonic fuselage configurations, and advanced control system designs.

The first X-1 is on permanent display in the National Air and Space Museum in Washington, DC. The second X-1, configured as the X-1E, is on display in front of the NASA Dryden Flight Research Center. The third X-1 was destroyed on 9 November 1951 at Edwards AFB, California.

X-1 Second Generation   Bell Aircraft Corporation

First Flight:	24 July 1951	**Sponsors:**	USAF, NACA
Last Flight:	23 January 1958	**Fastest Flight:**	Mach 2.44 (1,650 mph)
Total Flights:	54	**Highest Flight:**	90,440 feet

The X-1B was mainly used by the Air Force as a rocket research aircraft trainer, but under NACA auspices the aircraft had the honor of conducting the last second-generation X-1 flight. (NASA photo E-2539)

The second generation X-1s were designed to double the speed of sound and set altitude records in excess of 90,000 feet. Only the X-1A and X-1B were actually built—the X-1C, which was designed to test high-speed armaments, was cancelled before completion. The X-1D was destroyed during what was to be its first powered flight.

Possibly the most famous flight of the second generation X-1 series occurred on 12 December 1954 with Chuck Yeager at the controls of the X-1A. While flying at Mach 2.44 and 75,000 feet, the aircraft developed a slight left roll, but when Yeager attempted to correct, the aircraft snapped to the right and began a violent tumble toward earth. The pilot was rendered unconscious from being tossed about in the cockpit, and the aircraft continued out of control until Yeager regained consciousness and recovered at approximately 25,000 feet, an early example of inertial coupling.

The X-1A was destroyed after it was jettisoned following an inflight explosion over Edwards AFB on 8 August 1955. The X-1B is on permanent display at the Air Force Museum in Dayton, Ohio.

Bell Aircraft Corporation

X-1E

First Flight:	12 December 1955	**Sponsors:**	USAF, NACA
Last Flight:	6 November 1958	**Fastest Flight:**	Mach 2.24 (1,450 mph)
Total Flights:	26	**Highest Flight:**	75,000+ feet

The X-1E was modified from the second of the original first generation X-1 aircraft, and is shown here conducting a ground engine run at the Flight Research Center sometime during 1956. (Tony Landis Collection)

Despite the loss of the third X-1 and the X-1D, a requirement still existed for a higher performance X-1 so that the NACA could continue high-speed research. To satisfy this requirement, the second X-1 was almost completely rebuilt and redesignated the X-1E. Significant modifications included an updated canopy, ultra-thin wings (4 percent thickness/chord ratio), and a rocket assisted ejection seat.

The maximum altitude achieved by the X-1E was over 75,000 feet, and the top speed was Mach 2.24 (1,450 mph). During its test series, the X-1E demonstrated that the thin wing section was technically feasible for use on supersonic aircraft. An improved Reaction Motors XLR11, using a low-pressure turbopump, was also validated during X-1E test flights.

The aircraft was retired from service in November 1956 after 26 flights, and is now on permanent display in front of the NASA Dryden Flight Research Center.

X-2

Bell Aircraft Corporation

First Flight:	27 June 1952	**Sponsors:**	USAF
Last Flight:	27 September 1956	**Fastest Flight:**	Mach 3.196 (2,094 mph)
Total Flights:	20	**Highest Flight:**	125,907 feet

The X-2 was designed to explore flight at speeds and altitudes far beyond those attainable by the X-1s.
The X-2 was originally ordered under the designation XS-2. (NASA photo E-5749)

Two X-2s were built by Bell Aircraft at their Niagara Falls, New York, facility. The airframes were composed primarily of stainless steel and "K-Monel," an advanced lightweight heat-resistant steel alloy.

Like the X-1, the X-2 was air launched, this time from a Boeing B-50 bomber. Although plagued with a variety of problems, the X-2 program did produce a number of technological advances that helped pave the way for future high-speed, high-altitude aircraft. Among the most important was the use of high-strength steel alloys in aircraft construction—which gave rise to several innovative construction techniques and the development of specialized tooling. Additionally, the X-2 contributed to the continued understanding of high-Mach aerodynamics.

The first X-2 was dropped into Lake Ontario on 12 May 1953 following an explosion and fire that also caused extensive damage to the EB-50A launch aircraft. The second X-2 was lost in a crash on 27 September 1956 after setting an unofficial world speed record of Mach 3.196. The aircraft experienced "inertia coupling" resulting in complete loss of control—pilot Milburn Apt was killed in the accident. No examples of the X-2 survive.

Douglas Aircraft Company

X-3

First Flight:	20 October 1952	**Sponsors:**	USAF, NACA
Last Flight:	23 May 1956	**Fastest Flight:**	0.95 Mach (650 mph)
Total Flights:	51	**Highest Flight:**	35,000+ feet

The X-3 was designed to explore high speed aerodynamic phenomenon at speeds of Mach 2 for half an hour.
Unfortunately, a lack of suitable engines ultimately doomed the aircraft as a research tool. (NASA photo E-2412)

The X-3 Stiletto was a radical departure from the X-1 series and the X-2, and is one of the fastest looking aircraft ever designed. Built by Douglas Aircraft, the X-3 was jet powered and used conventional take-off and landing methods, instead of being air launched. Two X-3s were ordered. However, due to limited funding, lack of expected performance, and on-going engine difficulties, only one was completed for flight—the second was used for spare parts.

As a high-speed research aircraft, the X-3 was unquestionably a failure. It did, however, contribute somewhat to the understanding of the roll-coupling phenomenon, and pioneered the short-span low-aspect ratio wing used on several later aircraft. But the X-3's most significant contribution may have been in the field of aircraft landing gear, namely the tires. Because the X-3 had to achieve high speeds to maintain lift, take-off and landing speeds were very high (260 mph for takeoff, 200 mph for landing), and it was common for the tires to come apart. Several aircraft tire manufacturers used data gathered by the X-3 when developing new tires for high speed applications.

The X-3 is currently on display at the Air Force Museum in Dayton, Ohio.

X-4 Northrop Aircraft Corporation

First Flight:	16 December 1948	**Sponsors:**	USAF, NACA
Last Flight:	29 September 1953	**Fastest Flight:**	Mach 0.90 (630 mph) (approx)
Total Flights:	102	**Highest Flight:**	42,300 feet (approx)

The X-4 was the first U.S. effort to explore the transonic flight characteristics of tailless aircraft. The aircraft exhibited considerable pitch, roll, and yaw instabilities at approximately Mach 0.88. (Gerald Balzer Collection)

The Northrop X-4 was the first example of an X-vehicle intended to research something besides supersonic flight. The jet-powered X-4 was designed to evaluate the characteristics of a tailless aircraft at high subsonic speeds, a configuration believed to hold a great deal of promise for future aircraft.

Although not designed for supersonic speeds, the X-4 nevertheless proved that tailless swept-wing aircraft were not well suited for high transonic or supersonic performance. Pitch, roll, and yaw instabilities were very pronounced at speeds in excess of Mach 0.88, and there was no solution to the problem using the technology available at the time.

It is notable that both aircraft survived the flight test program, and there were no serious accidents during 102 flights. The first X-4 is currently on display at Edwards AFB. The second aircraft, after long being displayed at Maxwell AFB, Alabama, is currently at the Air Force Museum in Dayton, Ohio.

Bell Aircraft Corporation

X-5

First Flight:	20 June 1951	**Sponsors:**	USAF, NACA
Last Flight:	25 October 1955	**Fastest Flight:**	Mach 0.98 (705 mph) (approx)
Total Flights:	149	**Highest Flight:**	42,000 (approx)

The X-5s were the first high-performance variable-geometry wing aircraft to fly. The aircraft exhibited viscous spinning tendencies, but nevertheless accomplished all of the research goals originally envisioned. (Bell Aircraft via the Jay Miller Collection)

The X-5 was largely based on the design of the German Messerschmitt P.1101 which was captured near the end of World War II and brought to the United States for technical review and inspection. Two X-5s were manufactured by Bell, differing from their German ancestor primarily in being able to adjust their wing sweep angle in flight. The variable sweep wing could be adjusted from 20 to 60 degrees.

The first X-5 crashed on 13 October 1953, killing Air Force Major Raymond Popson. The other X-5 went on to a productive flight test career, in spite of the fact that the entire wing had to be translated fore-aft to maintain an acceptable center of gravity while the wing was being swept. The X-5 was the first successful variable-geometry aircraft and provided a great deal of data for programs such as the Grumman XF10F-1 and General Dynamics F-111.

The surviving X-5 was retired from service in 1955, and is now on display at the Air Force Museum in Dayton, Ohio.

X-6

Consolidated-Vultee Aircraft

First Flight:	Not Applicable	**Sponsors:**	USAF, AEC
Last Flight:	Not Applicable	**Fastest Flight:**	Not Applicable
Total Flights:	None	**Highest Flight:**	Not Applicable

The X-6s were to be used to evaluate the operational practicality of nuclear propulsion systems prior to committing to building a true nuclear-powered design. The X-6s were to be modified from two Convair B-36 Peacemakers. (Convair via the Jay Miller Collection)

Two Convair X-6s were ordered to evaluate the operational practicality of airborne nuclear propulsion systems prior to committing to building a prototype of a dedicated military design. The specific areas to be tested included crew shielding, propulsion, radiobiology, and the effects of radiation on various aircraft systems.

In addition to the X-6s, a single NB-36H was ordered to serve as an early flyable testbed. In the NB-36H, the nuclear reactor was functioning but provided no power to the aircraft itself. The X-6s would have been powered by a prototype airborne nuclear propulsion system installed in the aft bomb bays.

In the end, the X-6 program was cancelled before either of the two aircraft were built. The NB-36H was completed, however, making its first flight in September 1955. After conducting tests for approximately two years, the nuclear reactor was removed and the NB-36H was scrapped at Carswell AFB, Texas.

Lockheed Missiles & Space Co. X-7

First Flight:	26 April 1951	**Sponsors:**	USAF, USA, USN
Last Flight:	20 July 1960	**Fastest Flight:**	Mach 4.31 (2,881 mph)
Total Flights:	130	**Highest Flight:**	106,000 feet

The X-7 distinctively low aspect ratio wings had a thickness/chord ratio of only 4 percent. Small ailerons were mounted at the tips of the wing trailing edges, and the slab stabilator operated in pitch mode only. (Lockheed via the Jay Miller Collection)

The X-7 was designed as a research tool for high-speed ramjet propulsion systems. During the course of a successful flight test program that lasted over nine years, a large data base of ramjet test results was generated. There were four basic X-7 configurations: the X-7A-1 that was optimized for testing 20-28-inch diameter ramjets; the X-7A-3 that could accommodate larger engines; the X-7B that was similar in most respects to the X-7A-3 but was meant to test communications equipment; and the XQ-5 that was a dedicated high-speed, high-altitude target drone. In addition to basic engine research, the X-7s also tested various fuel additives and exotic fuel mixtures, such as boron-based propellants.

At least eight X-7s and XQ-5s are known to still exist. These include examples outside the NCO club in Sunnyvale, in the missile garden at White Sands; at Holloman AFB, New Mexico; at the Planes of Fame Museum in Chino, California; and at the Air Force Museum in Dayton, Ohio.

X-8

Aerojet General

First Flight: 24 April 1947

Last Flight: Unknown

Total Flights: 108

Sponsors: NACA, USAF, USN

Fastest Flight: Mach 6.0 (4,020 mph) (approx)

Highest Flight: 800,000 feet (approx)

The X-8 was conceived to fulfill a requirement for a relatively inexpensive upper air research vehicle and sounding rocket. Most X-8 flights were conducted at either the White Sands Missile Range, or nearby Holloman AFB, New Mexico. The missile was launched from a 143-foot high tower elevated at an angle of approximately 87 degrees.

The standard X-8 vehicle consisted of a payload section with the experimental package, a parachute recovery system, a liquid-fueled sustainer engine, stabilizing fins, and a solid-fueled booster engine.

The payloads carried by the X-8 varied considerably from mission to mission, but on the average weighed about 150 pounds. During the course of the X-8 program, data was obtained on high-altitude winds, solar radiation, high-altitude temperatures, cosmic radiation, the earth's magnetic field, warhead trajectories, effects of high-altitude on warhead design, propulsion anomalies at high altitudes, vehicle dynamics, and general atmospheric phenomenon.

A total of 108 vehicles were manufactured for both the Air Force and the Navy: 68 X-8s, 34 X-8As, 1 X-8B, 2 X-8Cs, and 3 X-8Ds. But perhaps more significantly, the type directly spawned the Aerobee sounding rocket, of which more than 800 were eventually manufactured and used by both military and civilian agencies around the country. Perhaps not surprisingly, no X-8s are known to have survived. However, numerous Aerobee rockets are on display around the country and are generally similar in appearance.

An X-8 accelerates from its launch tower at Holloman AFB under the power of its booster rocket. (William Pearson Collection via the Jay Miller Collection)

Bell Aircraft Corporation

X-9

First Flight:	28 April 1949	**Sponsors:**	USAF
Last Flight:	23 January 1953	**Fastest Flight:**	Mach 2.0 (1,300 mph) (approx)
Total Flights:	28	**Highest Flight:**	65,000 feet (approx)

This X-9 was later launched on 16 February 1951 over Holloman AFB, New Mexico, but its flight was cut short by a servo system malfunction. The area around the national insignia was day-glo orange. (Bell Aerospace via the Jay Miller Collection)

The X-9 Shrike (also designated the RTV-A-4) will remain perhaps the least heralded of all the early X-vehicles. Designed to serve as a testbed for the ill-fated GAM-63 Rascal air-to-surface missile, the X-9 was doomed to an unspectacular, but nevertheless productive, flight test career. The intent was to obtain aerodynamic, stability, guidance system, and propulsion data prior to proceeding into full-scale development of the Rascal.

The X-9 contributed significantly to the data base then being generated to support the air-to-surface missile programs. The vehicle provided useful insight into guidance and control system technology, and subsequently served as an instructional tool for engineering, maintenance, and support personnel. In addition, it was the first weapon of its kind to mate the potential of a liquid-fueled rocket engine with the destructive power of the atomic bomb. The missile served as a conceptual prototype for many later stand-off weapons such as the Hound Dog and Skybolt.

Although 93 X-9s were initially ordered, only 31 were actually delivered. None survived, and the only remaining identifiable piece is a large part of a vertical stabilizer in the Larry Bell Museum in Mentone, Indiana.

X-10

North American Aviation

First Flight:	14 October 1953	**Sponsors:**	USAF
Last Flight:	26 January 1959	**Fastest Flight:**	Mach 2.05 (1,350 mph) (approx)
Total Flights:	27	**Highest Flight:**	44,800 feet (approx)

The X-10 was an aerodynamic and systems testbed for the MX-770 (B/SM-64) Navaho Mach 3 intercontinental cruise missile. A total of 13 X-10s were manufactured, although only 10 were flown. (The Boeing Company Archives)

The primary mission of the X-10 was to serve as an aerodynamic and systems testbed for the cruise component of the SM-64 (B-64) Navaho missile. The X-10 was powered by a pair of Westinghouse J40 turbojet engines. At a later date, the X-10 itself was considered a cruise missile candidate, armed with a nuclear warhead and capable of taking off and flying to its target under its own power—but the successful development of the Atlas and Titan intercontinental ballistic missiles (ICBM) eliminated the need for such a weapon.

The X-10 successfully contributed to the development of the much larger Navaho missile, although that program would subsequently be cancelled in favor of the rocket-powered ICBMs. The X-10 verified the aerodynamics of the cruise component of the Navaho, as well as its complex navigation system.

Thirteen X-10s were manufactured, but only ten were flown—only a single example still survives, displayed at the Air Force Museum. An SM-65 Navaho missile is on display outside the gate at the Cape Canaveral AFS, Florida.

American X-Vehicles: An Inventory X-1 to X-50

Consolidated-Vultee Aircraft X-11

First Flight:	Not Applicable	**Sponsors:**	USAF
Last Flight:	Not Applicable	**Fastest Flight:**	Not Applicable
Total Flights:	None	**Highest Flight:**	Not Applicable

When the Atlas ICBM was being developed, Convair proposed constructing two incremental test vehicles to assist in verifying the enormous technological developments necessary to complete the program. At this point Atlas was envisioned as an enormous 160-foot high, 12-foot diameter missile weighing 440,000 pounds and powered by four booster engines and a single sustainer engine.

The first of these test vehicles was the X-11. Using an incremental flight test program, the X-11 would test the overall airframe using only the single sustainer engine while the subsequent X-12 would integrate more components including the four booster engines.

In the meantime, the national laboratories made breakthrough discoveries that allowed the nuclear payload for the Atlas to be drastically reduced in size. Based on the new estimates, Convair significantly reduced the size and weight of the Atlas ICBM, allowing the use of only three engines (two boosters and one sustainer) instead of the original five. The X-11 fell by the wayside.

Still, Convair wanted to proceed with an incremental test program, but this time the resultant vehicle was called the Atlas Series A (later shortened to simply Atlas A) instead of X-11. The test missile would be powered by the two booster engines; the sustainer would be added on the later Atlas B.

In the end, 16 Atlas As were built and 8 were launched from Cape Canaveral. They successfully demonstrated the pressure-stabilized propellant tanks and propulsion system components destined to equip the Atlas ICBM—which later became one of the premier space launch vehicles.

The last Atlas A (vehicle 16A) is launched at Cape Canaveral on 3 June 1958. The Atlas A was an early test version of the three-engine Atlas intercontinental ballistic missile that only used the two booster engines. This was very similar to what the X-11 would have accomplished for the earlier five-engine Atlas design. (USAF/45SW-HO via the Dennis R. Jenkins Collection)

X-12

Consolidated-Vultee Aircraft

First Flight:	Not Applicable	**Sponsors:**	USAF
Last Flight:	Not Applicable	**Fastest Flight:**	Not Applicable
Total Flights:	None	**Highest Flight:**	Not Applicable

The X-12 was envisioned as the second incremental test vehicle for the five-engine Atlas ICBM design. This vehicle would have added the four booster engines to the single sustainer previously tested on the X-11.

Like the X-11, the X-12 was to demonstrate the viability of the unique pressure-stabilized propellant tanks that were so thin they needed to be supported by internal pressure to keep them from collapsing. This construction technique greatly reduced the weight of the empty airframe, but brought its own set of concerns. The X-12 was also to demonstrate the radio-inertial guidance system and reentry (warhead) section being developed for Atlas.

When the Atlas was redesigned into a three-engine vehicle, the X-12 was dropped, although its place in the incremental test program was taken by the Atlas Series B.

The Atlas B was generally similar to the earlier Atlas A but incorporated the planned sustainer engine to prove the stage-and-a-half concept. A total of 13 vehicles were manufactured for flight and ground tests. All of the basic subsystems were tested in this series, including the MA-1 propulsion system, the Mod 1 radio guidance system, and the Mark 2 heat-sink reentry vehicle. The Atlas B series demonstrated booster staging and reentry vehicle separation, and attained a range of 6,500 miles with vehicle 12B.

One of the Atlas B (9B) test missiles is shown on Complex 11 at Cape Canaveral on 17 November 1958, just before it was launched. This flight would end in a propulsion system failure. (USAF/45SW-HO via the Dennis R. Jenkins Collection)

Ryan Aeronautical Company

X-13

First Flight:	10 December 1955	**Sponsors:**	USN, USAF
Last Flight:	30 July 1957	**Fastest Flight:**	483 mph (approx)
Total Flights:	Unknown (many)	**Highest Flight:**	10,000 feet (approx)

The X-13s were truly pioneers of jet-powered vertical flight, proving that VTOL flight, on jet thrust alone, was both technically feasible and practical. The ease with which the aircraft routinely transitioned from vertical to horizontal flight, and back again, left little question as to the flexibility and operational utility of such flight modes.
(Teledyne Ryan via the Jay Miller Collection)

The X-13 was designed to explore the feasibility of building a pure-jet vertical takeoff and landing (VTOL) fighter aircraft. Secondary purposes included validating several Ryan-designed VTOL control system concepts. The diminutive X-13 was powered by a single Rolls-Royce Avon turbojet engine.

The success and efficiency of the X-13 flight test program remains a high water mark in the history of research aircraft development. They provided a significant amount of data to the designers of subsequent VTOL aircraft designs. The X-13s proved that vertical flight, on jet thrust alone, was both technically feasible and practical. The ease with which the aircraft routinely transitioned from vertical to horizontal attitude, and back again, left little question as to the flexibility and operational utility of such flight modes.

Perhaps the only significant failing of the program was its lack of success in generating a follow-on production effort. This was due mainly to the aircraft's small size and limited payload capacity—and the inability of existing turbojet engines to power a larger version.

Both X-13s survived their test program. The first aircraft is on loan from the National Air and Space Museum to the San Diego Aerospace Museum in California. The second aircraft is on display at the Air Force Museum in Dayton, Ohio.

X-14

Bell Aircraft Corporation

First Flight:	17 February 1957	**Sponsors:**	USAF, NASA
Last Flight:	29 May 1981	**Fastest Flight:**	172 mph
Total Flights:	Unknown (many)	**Highest Flight:**	18,000 feet (approx)

The X-14 was used to verify that the concept of using vectored thrust in a VTOL aircraft was practical. Sir Stanley Hooker would later use this data when designing the Hawker P.1127 (Harrier prototype). (Bell Aerospace via the Jay Miller Collection)

The X-14 was another X-Plane dedicated to exploring vertical flight. The X-14 was originally created to explore the feasibility of operating a VTOL aircraft from a normal pilot station using standard flight instruments and references. Of equal importance, the X-14 was to demonstrate various VTOL systems and engine technologies—the aircraft was the first to demonstrate the concept of using vectored jet thrust as the only power system.

The X-14 successfully demonstrated that the concept of vectored jet thrust was viable, as subsequently used on the BAe/McDonnell Douglas Harrier. Flight tests using the X-14's variable stability control system resulted in major contributions to the understanding of V/STOL handling characteristics. The X-14 also proved useful as a testbed for various unique V/STOL concepts, such as NASA's direct side-force maneuvering system.

Over 25 pilots from around the world "previewed" V/STOL handling qualities in the X-14 prior to making test flights in other V/STOL designs. The single X-14 continued flying for nearly a quarter century before being retired to the Army Aviation Museum at Fort Rucker, Alabama. It is currently in storage at a private collection in Indiana.

North American Aviation

X-15

First Flight:	08 June 1959	**Sponsors:**	USAF, NACA/NASA, USN
Last Flight:	24 October 1968	**Fastest Flight:**	Mach 6.06 (4,018 mph)
Total Flights:	177	**Highest Flight:**	354,200 feet

Until the advent of the Space Shuttle, the X-15 was the fastest and highest flying manned winged vehicle, and several Air Force pilots earned Astronaut Wings for flights during the X-15 program. (NASA photo E-7419)

The X-15 was arguably the most successful high-speed flight research program ever undertaken. The X-15 was constructed specifically to explore the hypersonic (Mach 5+) flight regime, along with the necessary structures, propulsion systems, and control techniques. Although widely discounted at the time, a secondary purpose of the original X-15 program was to explore the possibilities of flight outside the sensible atmosphere.

The aircraft proved remarkably flexible as a research tool. In fact, most of the later flights used the X-15 as a carrier vehicle for other experiments rather than as a research aircraft in its own right. An assortment of experiments were carried, including micrometeorite collection pods, missile detection systems, samples of insulation destined for the Saturn launch vehicle, and a wide variety of others. The aircraft itself demonstrated a large, man-rated throttleable rocket engine, Inconel X heat-sink construction, and an advanced adaptive control system.

Of the three X-15s manufactured, one was rebuilt as the X-15A-2 after an accident, one crashed while returning from space—killing test pilot Major Michael J. Adams, and one survives in the National Air and Space Museum.

X-15A-2 North American Aviation

First Flight:	25 June 1964	**Sponsors:**	USAF, NASA
Last Flight:	3 October 1967	**Fastest Flight:**	Mach 6.70 (4,520 mph)
Total Flights:	22	**Highest Flight:**	249,000 feet

With Major William J. "Pete" Knight at the controls, the modified X-15A-2 set an unofficial speed record of 4,520 mph (Mach 6.70) on 3 October 1967. This would be the fastest flight of the X-15 program. (North American via the Jay Miller Collection)

Before the end of 1961, the X-15 had attained its Mach 6 design goal and flown well above 200,000 feet; by the end of 1962 the X-15 was routinely flying above 300,000 feet. The X-15 had already extended the range of winged aircraft flight speeds from Mach 3.2 to Mach 6.04, the latter achieved by Bob White on 9 November 1961.

A year later, on 9 November 1962, the second X-15 crashed while executing an emergency landing on Mud Lake near Edwards AFB. Pilot Jack McKay was seriously injured but later returned to flight status. The X-15 itself was nearly a write-off, but eventually the Air Force and NASA decided to rebuild it to a slightly different configuration. The fuselage was lengthened and external drop tanks were added to accommodate additional propellants. It was hoped this would allow the X-15A-2 to achieve at least Mach 7 while testing experimental scramjet engines. Using an ablative coating to provide additional heat protection, Major Pete Knight took the X-15A-2 to Mach 6.70 (4,520 mph) on 3 October 1967, the fastest piloted flight of the X-Plane program.

Due to damage resulting from this flight, the aircraft was retired and subsequently transferred to the Air Force Museum.

Bell Aircraft Corporation

X-16

First Flight:	None	**Sponsors:**	USAF
Last Flight:	Not Applicable	**Fastest Flight:**	Not Applicable
Total Flights:	Not Applicable	**Highest Flight:**	Not Applicable

The X-16 was designed as a high-altitude reconnaissance aircraft, but was ultimately cancelled in favor of the Lockheed U-2. A full-scale mockup was completed, but no aircraft were actually built. (Bell Aerospace via the Jay Miller Collection)

The X-16 was the most blatant misuse of the X-vehicle designation system—it was simply an attempt to hide what would today be called a spy-plane. The X-16 was designed to be a high-altitude long-range reconnaissance aircraft. A total of 28 aircraft were ordered, but none would be completed before the Lockheed U-2 successfully demonstrated its ability to perform the spy mission. The first X-16 was reportedly over 80 percent complete when it was cancelled.

The X-16 was a designer's nightmare—the wing was an extremely long-span high-aspect ratio unit that was significantly lighter and more flexible than any in existence at the time. In fact, the entire airframe was extremely flexible—a result of the need to make the aircraft as light as possible to allow it to achieve its 70,000-foot mission altitude. A 3,000 mile unrefueled range was predicted for the production aircraft.

Although never built, the X-16 pioneered several notable advances in lightweight structure design, and also was the driving force behind the development of high-altitude versions of the J57 jet engine that would go on to power the U-2 and other aircraft.

X-17 Lockheed Missiles & Space Co.

First Flight:	17 April 1956	**Sponsors:**	USAF, USN
Last Flight:	22 August 1957	**Fastest Flight:**	Mach 14.4 (9,504 mph)
Total Flights:	34	**Highest Flight:**	500,000 feet (approx)

The X-17 was a multistage rocket used to transport various reentry vehicle configurations to very high altitudes so that their flight characteristics could be examined in a natural environment. The original program objectives included operation at speeds in excess of Mach 15 and Reynolds Numbers of 24 million.

The X-17 proved to be one of the most significant missile programs during the 1950s. Its research into reentry characteristics contributed to the development of the warheads for the early intercontinental ballistic missiles, as well as to the early piloted space program capsules.

Perhaps more importantly, the X-17 produced the first realistic data ever obtained on heat transfer at extremely high Mach numbers and Reynolds numbers. Particularly valuable was the information generated relating to the hypersonic airflow around various blunt-body shapes as they made the transition from laminar to turbulent conditions.

A total of 26 X-17s were completed and tested, and as many as 7 others were later constructed from spare parts under Project Argus. No flightworthy X-17s survived, but what is presumably a structural test vehicle is on display at the Air Force Museum in Dayton, Ohio.

The X-17 used solid rocket motors to carry reentry vehicles to altitude. The original program objectives included reentry speeds of Mach 15 and Reynolds Numbers as high as 24 million. (U.S. Air Force via the Jay Miller Collection)

Hiller Aircraft Corporation # X-18

First Flight:	20 November 1959	**Sponsors:**	USAF, USN
Last Flight:	July 1961	**Fastest Flight:**	253 mph
Total Flights:	20	**Highest Flight:**	35,300 feet

The X-18 was built to investigate the feasibility of a large tilt-wing transport. Unlike the current Bell V-22 Osprey, the entire wing (and the engine assemblies) on the X-18 translated to vertical to support V/STOL flight. (Fairchild via the Jay Miller Collection)

The X-18 was conceived to assess the feasibility and practicality of a large tilt-wing V/STOL aircraft. The primary objectives were to investigate major problem areas associated with the tilt-wing concept while establishing criteria for the possible future development of similar aircraft.

Although its flight test program was short and inconclusive, the X-18 was nevertheless the first large aircraft to investigate the tilt-wing concept. An engine failure on the 20th flight prematurely terminated the flight test program. Data from this program was used during the design and development of the Vought XC-142 experimental transport aircraft in the early 1960s.

Only a single X-18 was completed—interestingly it used the fuselage from the Chase YC-122C and two turboprop engines that were surplused from the Navy's cancelled VTOL fighter program (Lockheed XFV-1 and Convair XFY-1 Pogo). No definitive information has been uncovered concerning the aircraft's ultimate fate, but it is generally assumed to have been scrapped at Edwards AFB.

X-19

Curtiss-Wright Corporation

First Flight:	20 November 1963	**Sponsors:**	USAF, USA, USN
Last Flight:	25 August 1965	**Fastest Flight:**	454 mph
Total Flights:	50	**Highest Flight:**	25,600 feet

The X-19 was the spiritual predecessor of the V-22 and demonstrated the feasibility of tilt-rotor aircraft. The power available from existing engines dictated the use of four powerplants and rotors/propellers. (Curtiss-Wright via the Jay Miller Collection)

Originally developed as a private venture by Curtiss-Wright, the X-19 was intended to demonstrate the practicality of the tilt-rotor concept. The X-19 was also used to explore the general feasibility of VTOL operations for such missions as the evacuation of personnel, missile site support, delivery of high priority cargo, counter-insurgency operations, reconnaissance, and close support operations.

Within the limited flight envelope explored by the X-19 prior to its demise, the aircraft demonstrated the general feasibility of the tandem tilt-rotor concept. The program successfully verified the dynamic and longitudinal stability, hover, and transition performance of the basic design. Although the tandem tilt-rotor design would not find further application, much of the data proved useful during the development of the XV-15 and later V-22 tilt-rotor aircraft.

Two X-19s were built—the first was destroyed in an accident on 25 August 1965, and the second aircraft was never completed. After all the useable components from the second aircraft were removed, the airframe was stored at the Aberdeen Proving Grounds and is currently in poor shape; it has been allocated to the Martin Museum in Maryland.

The Boeing Company

X-20

First Flight:	None	**Sponsors:**	USAF
Last Flight:	Not Applicable	**Fastest Flight:**	Not Applicable
Total Flights:	Not Applicable	**Highest Flight:**	Not Applicable

The X-20 Dyna-Soar was cancelled prior to the first flight vehicle being completed. The initial objective was to launch the Dyna-Soar on a Titan III booster to fill both experimental and, possibly, operational roles. (Boeing via the Dennis R. Jenkins Collection)

The X-20 Dyna-Soar was designed to provide a piloted maneuverable vehicle for conducting flight research in the hypersonic and flight regime. The X-20 was the final outgrowth of concepts that had begun with Eugen Sänger in 1928 and progressed through the Bell BoMi and RoBo concepts of the 1950s. At some points during its development, the Dyna-Soar was intended to be a quasi-operational system.

Although the X-20 never progressed beyond the preliminary construction stage, it effectively served as a testbed for a variety of advanced technologies that contributed enormously to various follow-on projects, including the Space Shuttle. In addition, numerous subsystems designed for Dyna-Soar found their way into later X-15 flight research.

The X-20 program was cancelled before the first vehicle was completed. Most of the subsystems manufactured for the uncompleted vehicle were used for various ground tests. Very few vehicles have contributed more to the science of very high-speed flight—especially vehicles that were never actually built.

X-21A

Northrop Corporation

First Flight:	18 April 1963	**Sponsors:**	USAF
Last Flight:	1964	**Fastest Flight:**	560 mph (approx)
Total Flights:	Unknown	**Highest Flight:**	42,500 feet (approx)

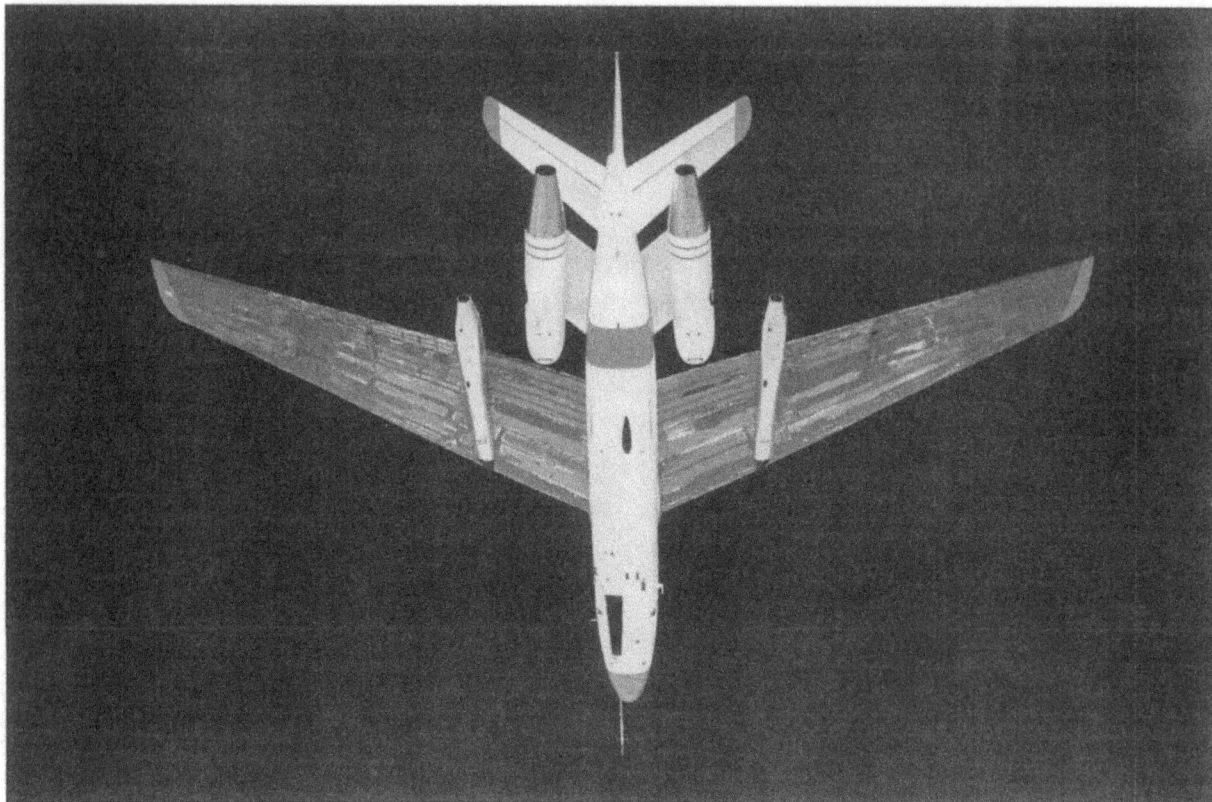

The two X-21As did not much resemble the Douglas WB-66D Destroyer light bombers they had been modified from, and were equipped with a completely new wing and engine nacelles that were hung on either side of the aft fuselage. (AFFTC History Office)

The X-21A was designed to explore the feasibility of utilizing full-scale boundary layer control on a large aircraft. Paper and wind tunnel studies conducted by Northrop had indicated boundary layer control would offer numerous performance benefits. After successfully demonstrating the ability to achieve laminar flow over approximately 75 percent of the wing surface, the X-21As were used to explore the impact of rain, sleet, snow, and other weather anomalies on the system.

During the flight test program, the X-21As demonstrated that the boundary layer control technique, called laminar flow control, was both effective and viable. However, they also showed that these benefits came at a significant maintenance penalty—the numerous small slots required for the airflow constantly plugged up.

The two X-21As were originally built as Douglas WB-66D light bomber derivatives that had been retired from active service. Both X-21As survived the flight test program and are currently in a bad state of repair on the photo range at Edwards AFB.

Bell Aerospace Textron

X-22

First Flight:	17 March 1966	**Sponsors:**	USN, USA, USAF
Last Flight:	1988	**Fastest Flight:**	255 mph
Total Flights:	500+	**Highest Flight:**	27,800 feet (approx)

The X-22A made a number of significant contributions to aerospace science, not the least of which was its exploration of V/STOL technologies and its use as a V/STOL aircraft analog. (Bell Aerospace via the Jay Miller Collection)

The X-22A was intended to evaluate a unique dual tandem ducted-propeller configuration for a V/STOL transport aircraft. It was also, from the beginning, designed to provide a highly versatile platform capable of general research on V/STOL handling qualities using a unique variable stability control system. The flight test program was undertaken by Calspan Corporation, in Buffalo, New York, under the auspices of the U.S. Navy. After demonstrating its basic handling qualities, most of the X-22A flights were oriented towards advancing the science of V/STOL flight, not the specific aircraft configuration itself. By the end of its long-lived test program, the X-22A had made a number of contributions, but perhaps the most significant was its ability to serve as a V/STOL analog for various advanced sensors and instrumentation destined for other V/STOL aircraft. The ducted-fan configuration itself proved quite workable, although it has not been selected for any further aircraft to date.

Two X-22As were built. The first was damaged beyond economical repair on 8 August 1966, and it was cannibalized to keep the second aircraft flying, although the fuselage was retained for a considerable time for use as a ground simulator at Calspan. The second aircraft is on display at the Niagara Aerospace Museum in New York.

X-23

Martin Marietta Corporation

First Flight:	21 December 1966	**Sponsors:**	USAF
Last Flight:	19 April 1967	**Fastest Flight:**	16,500 mph (reentry) (approx)
Total Flights:	3	**Highest Flight:**	500,000 feet (approx)

The X-23A, also known as the SV-5D, was designed to acquire data relating to lifting maneuverable reentry vehicles in support of several Air Force and NASA programs. The effort was under the auspices of project PRIME (precision recovery including maneuvering entry) and was part of the larger three-part START (spacecraft technology and advanced reentry test) program.

Under these programs, the same SV-5 lifting-body shape was tested at both extremes of its speed range—X-23A tested the very-high speed reentry phase; X-24A tested the low-speed landing characteristics. To study the effects of reentry on the ablative heat shield, the X-23A vehicle was intended to be recovered in mid-air by parachute.

The X-23A represented a major step forward in understanding the requirements imposed by atmospheric reentry on a maneuvering vehicle. Additionally, information was gathered on the effectiveness of its ablative heat shield, and on the possibility of refurbishing such a heat shield for multiple uses. The information derived from the X-23A program assisted the designers of the Space Shuttle and various maneuvering warhead projects in determining their requirements.

Four X-23As were manufactured, and three were launched using SLV-3 Atlas launch vehicles from SLC-3E at Vandenberg AFB, California. The first two vehicles were not recovered, but the third was and is currently on display at the Air Force Museum. There is no record of the disposition of the fourth vehicle.

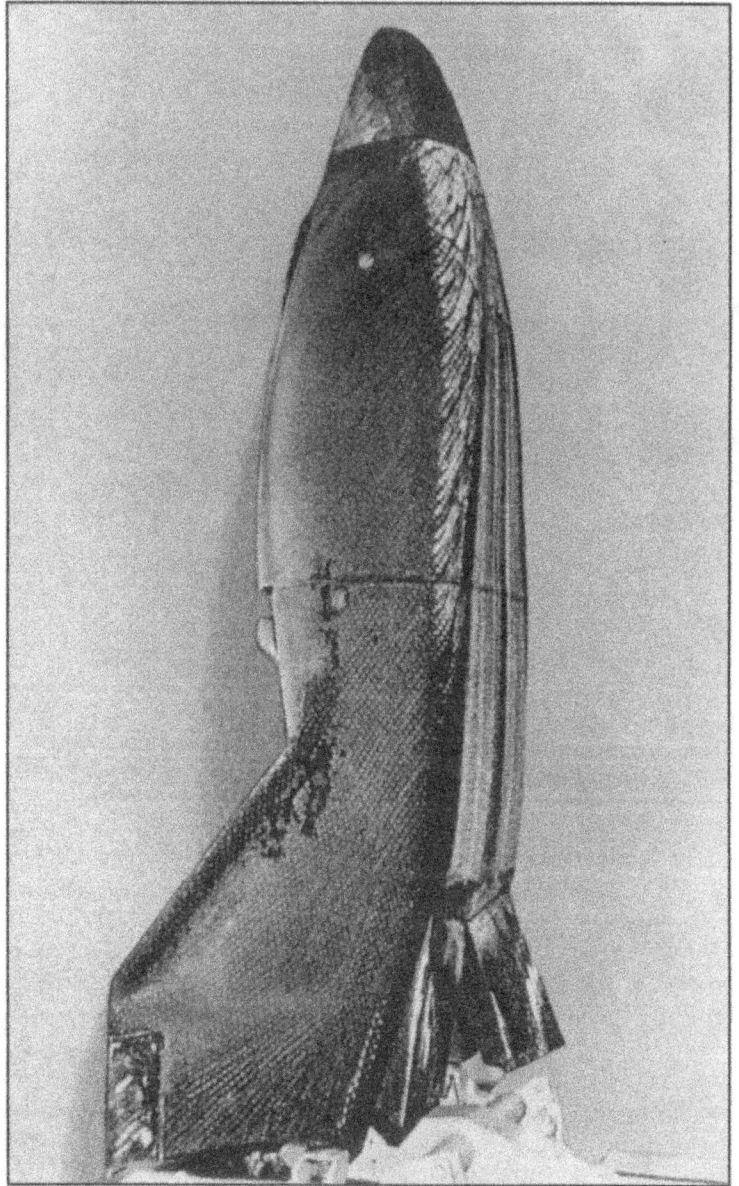

The X-23A/SVD-5D program represented a major step forward in the design of maneuvering reentry vehicles, and provided valuable data for the eventual design of the Space Shuttle orbiter. This is the recovered third X-23A, currently on display at the Air Force Museum. (Martin Marietta via the Jay Miller Collection)

Martin Marietta Corporation X-24A

First Flight:	17 April 1969	**Sponsors:**	USAF, NASA
Last Flight:	4 June 1971	**Fastest Flight:**	Mach 1.60 (1,036 mph)
Total Flights:	28	**Highest Flight:**	71,400 feet

The shape of the X-24A was essentially an enlarged X-23A. Unlike the X-23A, which was designed to explore high-speed flight, the X-24A was designed to explore the low-speed and landing stability of the design. (Martin Marietta via the Jay Miller Collection)

The X-24A/SV-5P represented the low-speed end of the test spectrum for the START program that had also tested the X-23A. The X-24A was used in project PILOT (piloted low-speed tests). The rocket-powered X-24A was specifically designed to explore the low-speed flight characteristics of a maneuverable lifting-body design. The design was essentially identical to the SV-5D used in project PRIME as the X-23A, allowing both ends of the flight spectrum to be tested on the same shape. The X-24A decisively demonstrated that lifting-bodies could consistently make precision landings onto a hard runway, proving the concept for the future Space Shuttle.

Only a single X-24A was manufactured, but two extremely similar jet-powered SV-5Js were also built. The SV-5Js were to be powered by a single J60 turbojet engine and used as trainers to introduce pilots to the low-speed handling characteristics of lifting-bodies, but in the end neither aircraft ever flew. One of the SV-5Js is on display at the Air Force Academy near Colorado Springs, Colorado, while the other has been superficially modified into an X-24A and is on display at the Air Force Museum. The X-24A itself was heavily modified to become the X-24B.

X-24B Martin Marietta Corporation

First Flight:	1 August 1973	**Sponsors:**	USAF, NASA
Last Flight:	9 September 1975	**Fastest Flight:**	Mach 1.76 (1,164 mph)
Total Flights:	36	**Highest Flight:**	74,140 feet

Underneath the sleek skin of the X-24B lurked the original X-24A. The streamlined shape was designed by the Air Force Flight Dynamics Laboratory as the FDL-7/FDL-8. (Martin Marietta via the Jay Miller Collection)

Although the X-24A program successfully met all of its objectives, engineers and scientists at the Air Force Flight Dynamics Laboratory (FDL) wanted to conduct similar tests on an even more advanced lifting-body shape called the FDL-7/FDL-8. The original plan was to convert one of the jet-powered SV-5Js into the advanced testbed, but since this would have entailed extensive modifications to fit a rocket engine in place of the turbojet, these plans were shelved. As the rocket-powered X-24A was nearing the end of its test program, it was finally decided to utilize it instead since the modifications were expected to be less extensive.

Underneath the sleek shell of the X-24B lived the original X-24A—the new skin was essentially "gloved on" to the original aircraft. Most systems were retained intact. Although the X-24B was intended to evaluate the flight characteristics of the FDL-7 shape, in reality it spent most of its 36 flights demonstrating precision landing techniques that would be used on the forthcoming Space Shuttle. When Bill Dana completed the X-24B's final flight on 9 September 1975, it marked the end of rocket-powered research aircraft at Edwards—at least for 25 years. The X-24B is currently on display at the Air Force Museum, alongside one the the SV-5Js configured as the X-24A.

Bensen Aircraft Corporation

X-25

First Flight:	5 June 1968	**Sponsors:**	USAF
Last Flight:	1968	**Fastest Flight:**	85 mph
Total Flights:	Unknown	**Highest Flight:**	12,500 feet

A small 4-cylinder air-cooled McCulloch piston engine mounted directly behind the pilot powered the rotor system of the X-25A. Three different versions of the X-25 were manufactured. (Bensen Aircraft via the Jay Miller Collection)

The X-25 program was begun in response to a perceived need for an emergency egress capability for downed pilots. The vehicle was part of the Air Force's Discretionary Descent Vehicle (DDV) program intended to give aircrew members forced to abandon their aircraft an option of landing somewhere other than where wind and gravity dictated.

The concept was to equip combat aircraft with a small ultralight autogyro that could be used by the aircrew. To test the concept, modified versions of the well-known Bensen autogyro were ordered, and three vehicles were manufactured—an X-25, X-25A, and X-25B. The basic X-25 was termed a "gyro-chute" and was unpowered. It was intended for one-time use and had a rotor system designed for automatic blade deployment at any ejection speed, including supersonic. As far as is known, no piloted tests were ever conducted with this vehicle. The other two X-25s were used to evaluate piloting techniques and training requirements of the autogyro. The end of the war in Vietnam caused the Air Force to lose interest in the DDV concept, and no full-scale operational tests were ever conducted.

An X-25A is at the Air Force Museum in Dayton, Ohio, and an X-25B is at the AFFTC Museum at Edwards AFB.

X-26

Lockheed / Schweizer

First Flight:	3 July 1962	**Sponsors:**	DARPA, USA, USN
Last Flight:	1973	**Fastest Flight:**	158 mph
Total Flights:	Unknown (many)	**Highest Flight:**	18,500 feet

The X-26As were unpowered gliders used by the Navy Test Pilot School. This is an X-26B, a powered derivative used as a stealthy observation aircraft. (Lockheed via the Jay Miller Collection)

The X-26A was a Schweizer SGS 2-32 sailplane that was used by the Navy to expose novice pilots to the phenomenon of yaw/roll coupling. Conventional jet trainers reacted much too quickly and dangerously for effective instruction—an aircraft that had unusually slow roll rates and excellent recovery characteristics was needed instead. Four of the gliders were originally delivered, but accidents soon claimed three of them. In each case the aircraft was replaced with a new one, and the training program continues to this day, making the X-26 the longest-lived X-vehicle.

The Lockheed X-26B was created in response to a requirement for a stealth-type observation aircraft in Vietnam. Two of the Navy X-26A aircraft were temporarily modified with small engines and slow-speed propellers, and were eventually equipped with a variety of intelligence-gathering sensors. Testing in Vietnam was evidently successful as 14 further aircraft were acquired under various designations, including 11 YO-3As. The original X-26As were demodified and returned to the Navy after the construction of the YO-3As. At least one of the YO-3As was later used by NASA as an acoustical signature research tool. One X-26B and a YO-3A are preserved in the Army Aviation Museum at Fort Rucker, Alabama.

Lockheed-California Company   X-27

First Flight:	None	**Sponsors:**	Lockheed-California
Last Flight:	Not Applicable	**Fastest Flight:**	Not Applicable
Total Flights:	Not Applicable	**Highest Flight:**	Not Applicable

The X-27 was a major modification of the Lockheed F-104 Starfighter designed as an advanced lightweight fighter for foreign sales. The project did not progress beyond the mockup stage when the U.S. Air Force declined to purchase a version of the aircraft. (Lockheed via the Jay Miller Collection)

The X-27 Lancer program can trace its roots to a Lockheed desire to develop a replacement for the F-104 Starfighter that was in wide service around the world. Lockheed's goal was to create a new aircraft with considerably improved performance while maintaining significant commonality with the F-104 to ease maintenance and training concerns.

The X-27 was conceived as the prototype of the desired advanced lightweight fighter and was based on the CL-1200 Lancer design developed by the Lockheed Skunk Works. The program, however, failed to obtain any significant congressional or DoD support, and no actual aircraft were built. Nevertheless, a full-scale mockup was completed.

In the end, the X-27 program was a lesson in political maneuvering as much as technological advances. Lockheed's Kelly Johnson almost managed to get official backing of a commercial program, but in the end was defeated by military services that did not want to see competition for the funding necessary to complete the F-14 and F-15 programs.

Eventually the Air Force and Navy would embrace the lightweight fighter concept with the F-16 and (sort of) F/A-18, but Lockheed would not be a participant.

X-28

George Pereira / Osprey Aircraft

First Flight:	12 August 1970	**Sponsors:**	USN
Last Flight:	22 October 1971	**Fastest Flight:**	135 mph
Total Flights:	Unknown	**Highest Flight:**	18,000 feet

The X-28A was equipped with a simple constant-chord wing. The entire trailing edge, except for a small area near the root, was occupied by flaps and ailerons. The small size of the cockpit is noteworthy. (Howard Levy via the Jay Miller Collection)

The homebuilt Osprey I was ordered by the Navy as the X-28 in response to a study that indicated the potential usefulness of a small single-engine seaplane for police-type duties in Southeast Asia. The Naval Air Development Center acquired the aircraft as part of the Air Skimmer program. The only requirements levied on the program were that the aircraft be small, lightweight, capable of VFR flight, able to be manufactured in Southeast Asia without a major tooling investment, and cost under $5,000 when purchased in quantity.

The Navy evaluation of the X-28A showed that it was generally easy to fly and that most pilots would have no trouble mastering it. Performance was considered exceptionally good considering its 90 horsepower engine.

The single X-28 is currently at the Mid-America Air Museum in Sioux City, Kansas. Numerous other versions of the Osprey I design have been built by individuals around the country.

Grumman Aerospace Corporation X-29

First Flight:	14 December 1984	**Sponsors:**	DARPA, USAF, NASA
Last Flight:	30 September 1991	**Fastest Flight:**	Mach 1.8 (1,100 mph) (approx)
Total Flights:	437	**Highest Flight:**	55,000 feet (approx)

The X-29A proved many of the advantages of the forward swept wing, but also showed that the configuration generated a great deal more drag in some flight regimes than expected. (NASA photo EC91 491-7)

The concept of the forward swept wing had been tested during World War II, but when these early tests were conducted, strong lightweight materials were not readily available. It was not until the late 1970s and 1980s that new materials allowed reasonable testing to begin. Unfortunately, the perceived drag reductions were not realized.

Two X-29As were built and flown—each served as testbed for multiple missions including aerodynamics, composite building techniques, and advanced avionics. Although most X-29A flights were conducted from Edwards AFB, one X-29A was flown to the Dayton (Ohio) International Air Show and to the Experimental Aircraft Association's (EAA) International Convention and Sport Aviation Exhibition at Oshkosh, Wisconsin.

The first X-29 is at the Air Force Museum, and the second aircraft is on display at the Dryden Flight Research Center. The National Air and Space Museum has a full-scale X-29 mockup on display.

X-30

First Flight:	None	**Sponsors:**	DARPA, USAF, NASA
Last Flight:	Not Applicable	**Fastest Flight:**	Not Applicable
Total Flights:	Not Applicable	**Highest Flight:**	Not Applicable

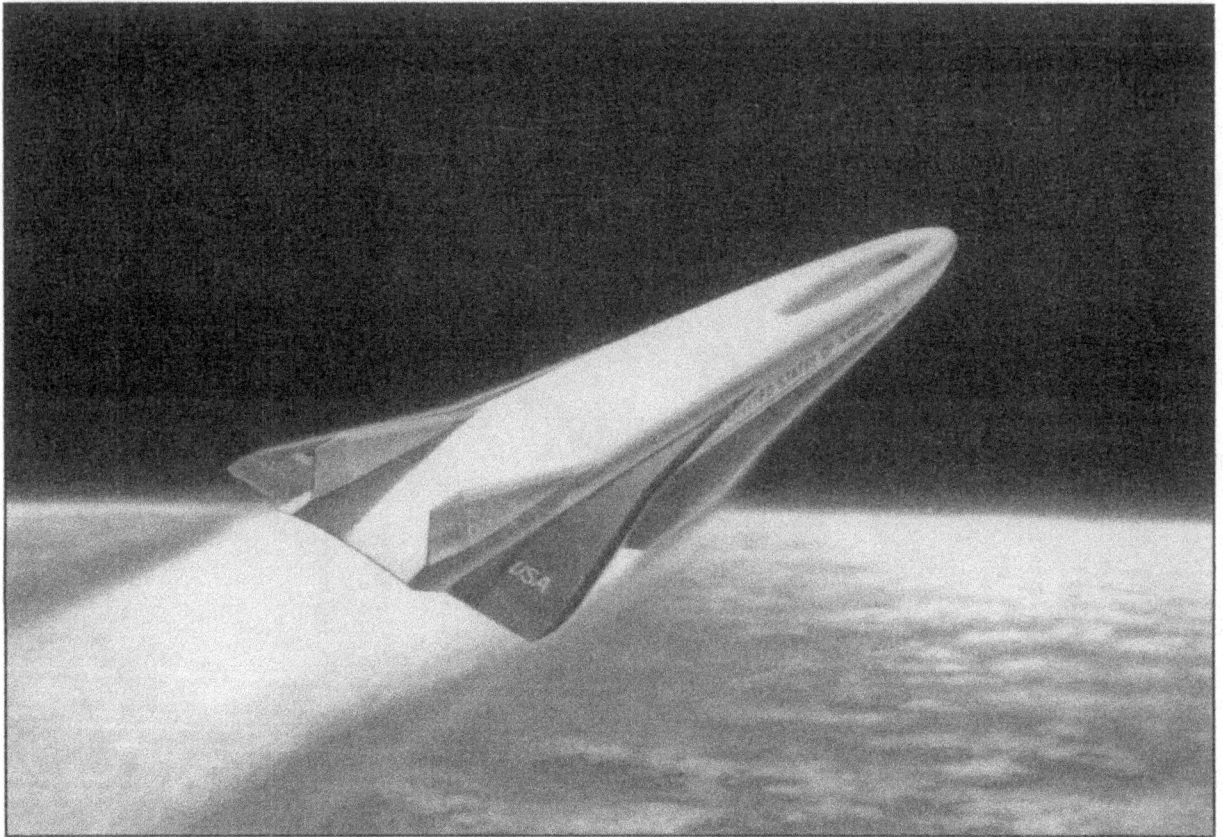

Begun as part of President Reagan's "Orient Express" initiative, the X-30 ultimately proved to be too advanced for the available budget. Nevertheless, the program did prove instrumental in developing a great many new technologies. (Dennis R. Jenkins Collection)

The program to develop what was called the National Aero-Space Plane (NASP) had its roots in a highly classified Defense Advanced Research Projects Agency (DARPA) project called Copper Canyon that ran from 1982 to 1985. Originally conceived as a feasibility study for a single-stage-to-orbit (SSTO) vehicle that could take off and land horizontally, Copper Canyon became the starting point for what Ronald Reagan called "… a new Orient Express that could, by the end of the next decade, take off from Dulles Airport and accelerate up to twenty-five times the speed of sound, attaining low earth orbit or flying to Tokyo within two hours…" It was not to be.

In an ambitious program that involved every major aerospace company in the United States, DARPA proposed building a prototype NASP designated X-30. Unfortunately, the X-30 ran into significant cost and technical difficulties, resulting in its cancellation. The Hypersonic Systems Technology Program (HySTP), initiated in late 1994, was designed to transfer the accomplishments made in hypersonic technologies by the NASP program into a technology development program. The X-43A Hyper-X is one of the results of the HySTP program.

Rockwell International / MBB

X-31

First Flight:	11 October 1990	**Sponsors:**	DARPA, USN, German MoD
Last Flight:	Not Applicable	**Fastest Flight:**	Mach 1.28 (900 mph)
Total Flights:	Ongoing	**Highest Flight:**	40,000 feet (approx)

The X-31 makes the first research flight of the Vector program at NAS Patuxent River, Maryland, on 17 May 2002.
The aircraft had been in storage for the previous six years. (U.S. Navy photo 020517-N-1431D-001)

The X-31 was designed to break the "stall barrier," allowing it to flight at angles of attack which would typically cause an aircraft to stall with a complete loss of control.To accomplish this, the X-31 employs thrust vectoring paddles that are located in the jet exhaust and small computer-controlled canards to help keep the aircraft stable at high attack angles.

The first X-31 was lost on 19 January 1995—the pilot, Karl Lang, ejected safely at 18,000 feet before the aircraft crashed. The second X-31 completed the 580th and last flight of its original research program on 13 May 1995 and was placed in storage. The aircraft was shipped to NAS Patuxent River in April 2000, where it was largely rebuilt for the Vector (Vectoring Extremely Short Take-Off and Landing Control Tailless Operation Research) program. The revised aircraft made its first flight for Vector on 24 February 2001. After two months of basic flight testing, the aircraft began a year of upgrading and ground testing to ready it for the current flight test period, in which it will perform ESTOL landings to a "virtual runway" at 5,000 feet. The X-31 took to the air again on 17 May 2002.

X-32

The Boeing Company

First Flight (X-32A):	18 September 2000	**Sponsors:**	USAF, USN, USMC, RAF
First Flight (X-32B):	7 March 2001	**Fastest Flight:**	1.5+ Mach (est.)
Total Flights (X-32A):	66	**Highest Flight:**	40,000+ feet (est.
(X-32B):	78		

The X-32A completed low- and high-speed taxi tests at Palmdale on 23 May 2000 in preparation for its first flight.
(Boeing via the Dennis R. Jenkins Collection)

The Joint Strike Fighter (JSF) has been described as the largest single defense program in history, with a potential market for 5,000-8,000 aircraft worth over $200 billion when all potential export orders are included. In November 1996 Boeing and Lockheed Martin were awarded contracts to build two Concept Demonstrator Aircraft (CDA— one CTOL version and one STOVL version—each. The aircraft were not intended to be fighter prototypes, but rather to prove that the selected design concepts would work, hence the use of X designations. Boeing was assigned X-32 (a number reserved for the earlier JAST program) while Lockheed Martin received the designation X-35.

The Boeing X-32 used a novel airframe shape combined with a direct-lift STOVL configuration. The Harrier-style direct lift concept required the lift nozzles to be on the center of gravity of the aircraft. To achieve this the engine was located in the front portion of the fuselage, with the vectoring nozzles immediately behind it, and then a long exhaust duct leading back to the afterburner and pitch-axis thrust vectoring nozzle at the rear. The engine position and overall dimension limitations dictated a very short nose.

The X-32A (right) and X-32B (below) during their test program. Regardless of the aircraft's performance potential, the general concensus was that it was the ugliest design to come from an American manufacturer in decades. One thing that worked against Boeing in the competition was that the X-32 design was not representative of the proposed production aircraft. (Tony Landis Collection)

For the two CDA aircraft, the designation X-32A was allocated to the CTOL version and X-32B to the STOVL version. Unlike the Lockheed Martin X-35, there were no airframe changes required to demonstrate U.S. Navy aircraft carrier (CV/CTOL) approach capabilities—the X-32A performed both roles.

The X-32A featured a non-moving intake and wide span wings with accentuated tip extensions. The X-32B featured a moving intake cowl that translated forward during hover to allow more air into the engine. The fuselage was slightly shorter and the wing span was narrower to reduce weight. After the X-32 design was frozen, the planned Model 375 production version continued to evolve, gaining a conventional horizontal stabilizer and a stubby swept wing rather than the original delta wing. The engine intake cowl was also raked backward rather than forward.

The Lockheed Martin X-35 was selected as the winning JSF design on 26 October 2001. Some JSF work may be awarded to Boeing as a consolation. The X-32s will eventually be donated to museums.

X-33 Lockheed Martin Corporation

First Flight:	None	**Sponsors:**	NASA, Lockheed Martin
Last Flight:	Not Applicable	**Fastest Flight:**	Not Applicable
Total Flights:	Not Applicable	**Highest Flight:**	Not Applicable

Although generally called a lifting body, the X-33 was its own unique shape. The mostly completed vehicle is currently in storage at its launch site near Haystack Butte on the Edwards AFB reservation. (Lockheed Martin via the Dennis R. Jenkins Collection)

The X-33 was a half-scale prototype of the proposed VentureStar® reusable launch vehicle (RLV). The X-33 was designed and built as part of a "cooperative agreement" between NASA and an industry team led by Lockheed Martin that included Boeing (Rocketdyne), B. F. Goodrich (formerly Rohr Industries), Honeywell (formerly AlliedSignal), and Sverdrup. The X-33 was a suborbital demonstrator and was never intended to reach orbit. Initially the vehicle was intended to reach velocities of Mach 15, although this was later reduced to Mach 12.

The X-33 was designed to demonstrate unique aerospike engines, composite liquid hydrogen tanks, a metallic thermal protection system, and an austere launch site environment. The development program ran into problems almost immediately, and the failure of the composite liquid hydrogen tanks during full-scale testing led to massive cost overruns during late 2000 and early 2001. As a result, NASA cancelled further funding for the X-33 in March 2001 after the vehicle was about 75 percent complete. This left Lockheed, who had already invested over $200 million of company funds in the project, free to complete and fly the X-33 alone, but the company elected not to do so.

American X-Vehicles: An Inventory X-1 to X-50

Orbital Sciences Corporation
X-34

First Flight:	None	**Sponsors:**	NASA
Last Flight:	Not Applicable	**Fastest Flight:**	Not Applicable
Total Flights:	Not Applicable	**Highest Flight:**	Not Applicable

The X-34 Technology Testbed Demonstrator on NASA Dryden ramp on 16 April 1999. The projected performance of the X-34 was essentially the same as the X-15 had achieved 40 years earlier. (NASA photo EC99-44976-31 by Tony Landis)

The X-34 was a reusable testbed vehicle designed to demonstrate technologies that were considered essential to lowering the cost of access to space. Specific technologies to be demonstrated by the X-34 included advanced composite structures, a composite RP-1 fuel tank, an advanced thermal protection system, and autonomous flight operations. The all-composite vehicle was designed for speeds up to Mach 8 and altitudes of 250,000 feet.

The first of three X-34 vehicles began captive-carry flights at Edwards AFB, in June 1999 using the L-1011 TriStar owned by Orbital Sciences. At this point the first flight was scheduled for late 2000. The initial free flights were to be made over the White Sands Missile Range, with the full-performance flights taking place over the Atlantic Ocean off the Kennedy Space Center in Florida. A special hangar was constructed at Kennedy to support the program, and was later used to house debris from the Space Shuttle *Columbia* accident. Although the program appeared to be progressing satisfactorily, revisions to the requirements led to significant cost growth and schedule slip. In March 2001 NASA cancelled the X-34 program before any of the aircraft had actually flown except under the L-1011.

X-35 Lockheed Martin Corporation

First Flight (X-35A):	24 October 2000	**Sponsors:**	USAF, USN, USMC, RAF
First Flight (X-35B):	24 June 2001	**Fastest Flight:**	Mach 1.22 (est.)
First Flight (X-35C):	16 December 2000	**Highest Flight:**	34,000 feet (est.)
Total Flights (X-35A):	27		
Total Flights (X-35B):	39		
Total Flights (X-35C):	73		

The first of the X-35 demonstrators. Despite being completely different, there is a strong family resemblance to the Lockheed F/A-22 Raptor. (Lockheed Martin via the Tony Landis Collection)

The X-35 was the Lockheed Martin Joint Strike Fighter (JSF) demonstrator, competing with the Boeing X-32. In November 1996 Boeing and Lockheed Martin were awarded contracts to build two Concept Demonstrator Aircraft (CDA)—one Conventional Take-Off and Landing (CTOL) version and one Short Take-Off and Vertical Landing (STOVL) version—each. The aircraft were not intended to be fighter prototypes, but rather to prove that the selected design concepts would work, hence the use of X-series designations.

Lockheed constructed two prototypes for the evaluation. The initial X-35A reflected the basic Air Force CTOL design, and was used for early flights before being modified into the STOVL version, designated X-35B. While Boeing proposed a direct lift STOVL design based on that used in the Harrier, Lockheed opted for a different approach in meeting the vertical flight requirements. Inspired by the Russian Yak-141, the X-35B incorporated a separate lift-fan that was shaft-driven by the F119 engine, allowing cooler exhaust temperatures during hover. While the Boeing design was more conventional, Lockheed argued that their strategy was better in the long term since it offered more

The X-35B during hover. Note the open doors on the top and bottom of the forward fuselage to support the lift-fan. The lift-fan was shaft-driven off the main engine, and initially caused a bit of worry due to bearing problems. The theory is that the relatively cold air being exhausted from the lift-fan (it is not an engine and burns no fuel) will be easier to deal with than the jet exhaust from the Harrier. (Tony Landis)

The X-35C demonstrator taxies at Palmdale prior to its first flight. Note the faceted intakes on the side of the fuselage and the colorful tail markings unique to the X-35C. (Lockheed Martin via the Tony Landis Collection)

room for growth as the aircraft evolves. The second airframe was the X-35C STOVL demonstrator for the Navy. This model featured an enlarged wing of greater span and area for larger fuel capacity as well as enlarged horizontal tails and flaperons for greater control effectiveness during low-speed carrier approaches.

The X-35 was selected as the winner of the JSF competition on 26 October 2001. The production aircraft, unexplainably, will be designated F-35. The System Development and Demonstration (SDD) phase of the F-35 JSF program started with the signing of the SDD contract in October 2001, and with the delivery of test aircraft scheduled to begin in 2008. During the SDD phase, 22 aircraft (14 flying test aircraft and 8 ground-test aircraft) will be produced and tested. The JSF program is slated to produce a total of 3,002 aircraft for the United States and United Kingdom armed forces, and possibly additional aircraft for new members Italy, Turkey, Canada, Denmark, Norway, and the Netherlands. Other countries have expressed an interest in joining the program and are expected to do so in the coming years. The program is potentially worth $200 billion after all the export orders are considered.

X-36

The Boeing Company

First Flight:	17 May 1997	**Sponsors:**	NASA, Boeing
Last Flight:	24 September 1997	**Fastest Flight:**	204 mph
Total Flights:	25	**Highest Flight:**	20,500 feet

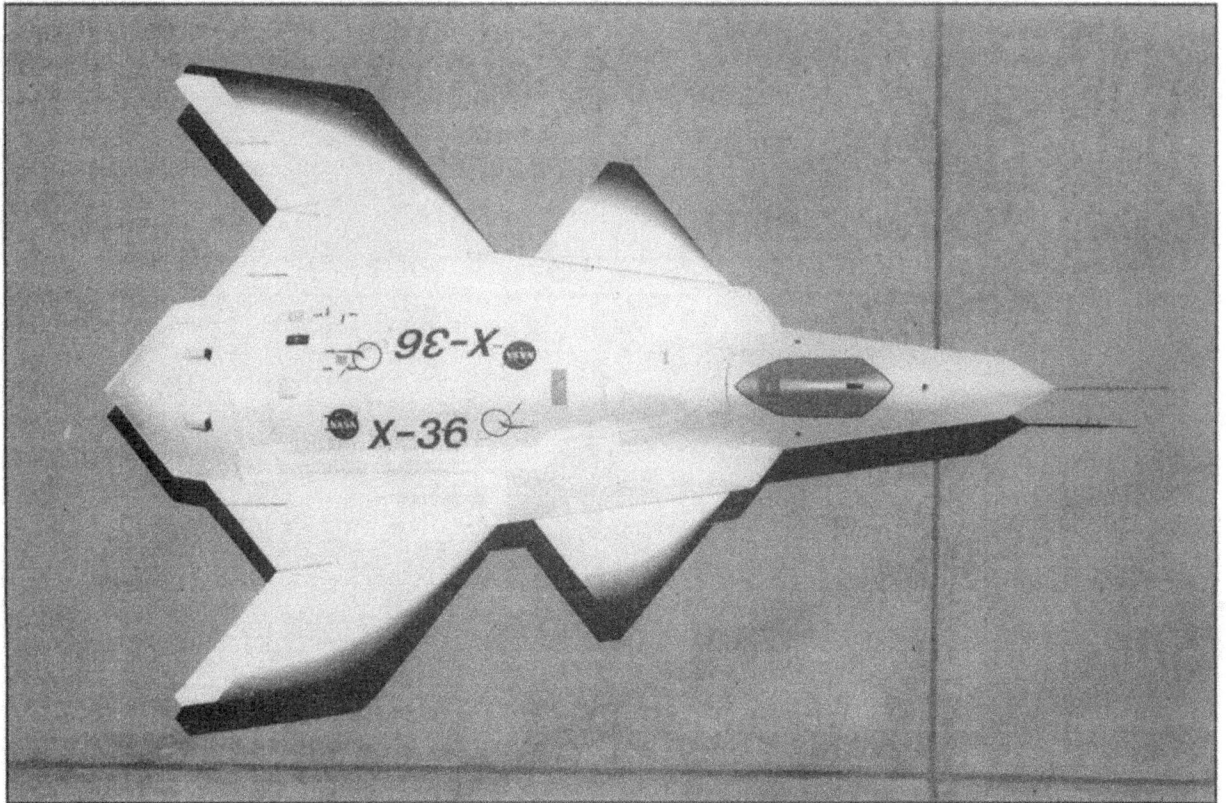

The X-36 vehicle photographed in July 1997. (NASA photo EC97-44165-151)

The 28-percent scale, remotely piloted X-36 had no vertical or horizontal tails, reducing the weight, drag, and radar cross section typically associated with traditional fighter aircraft. The X-36 also explored advanced flight control technologies, such as split ailerons and thrust vectoring. The ailerons not only split to provide yaw (left and right) control, but also raise and lower asymmetrically to provide roll control.

Boeing (formerly McDonnell Douglas) manufactured two X-36 vehicles, and the aircraft successfully completed all of its planned low- and high-g agility maneuvers, which demonstrated the aircraft's ability to quickly perform under a wide range of aerodynamic loads, and included 360-degree rolls at angles of attack (AoA) up to 15 degrees and rapid turning-rolling maneuvers at up to 35 degrees AoA.

Including the design and production of the two aircraft and flight testing, the total budget for the X-36 program was only $17 million. The first X-36 was shipped to the Air Force Museum in April 2003, and the second airframe is in storage at the Dryden Flight Research Center.

The Boeing Company

X-37

First Flight:	Pending	**Sponsors:**	NASA, USAF
Last Flight:	Not Applicable	**Fastest Flight:**	Not Applicable
Total Flights:	Not Applicable	**Highest Flight:**	Not Applicable

An artist concept of the X-37 Future-X Pathfinder vehicle in orbit. (NASA photo EC99-45145-2)

The X-37, formerly known as the Future-X Pathfinder, will make a series of atmospheric and orbital test flights to evaluate over 40 airframe, propulsion, and operations technologies designed to lower the cost of access to space. The X-37 will be launched aboard the Space Shuttle as a secondary payload—once on-orbit the Space Shuttle will deploy the X-37 from the payload bay. The X-37 is 27.5 feet long—about half the length of the Shuttle payload bay—and weighs about 12,000 pounds. The vehicle is designed to be capable of at least 20 flights and landings.

The X-37 shape is identical to the X-40A developed for the Air Force, and recently the two programs have essentially been merged with the lone X-40A now serving as a prototype for the X-37. The X-37 is scheduled to be delivered to the Dryden Flight Research Center in late 2003, and the first unpowered launch from a NASA B-52 is planned for 2004. The X-37 flights will permit testing of a wide variety of experiments and technologies to be evaluated under real-world conditions. These include a highly durable, high-temperature thermal protection system and important new aerodynamic features, all of which are applicable to future reusable space vehicles. The vehicle design also includes a small experiment bay to allow subsystem testing during the reentry flights.

X-38

NASA / Scaled Composites

First Flight:	12 March 1998	**Sponsors:**	NASA, ESA
Last Flight:	13 December 2001	**Fastest Flight:**	500 mph (approx)
Total Flights:	8	**Highest Flight:**	39,000 feet

X-38 ship #2 in free flight on 9 July 1999. (NASA photo EC99-45080-219 by Carla Thomas)

NASA originally called this the X-35, not realizing that the Air Force had already assigned that number. The X-38 was a concept demonstrator of a crew rescue vehicle (previously called an assured crew return vehicle—ACRV) for the International Space Station. The vehicles were designed in-house by the NASA Johnson Space Center with assistance from the Dryden Flight Research Center, and were manufactured by Scaled Composites.

The X-38 design used a lifting body concept originally developed by the Air Force's X-24A in the mid-1960s. Following the jettison of a deorbit engine module, the X-38 would glide from orbit unpowered like the Space Shuttle and then use a steerable parafoil parachute, a technology developed by the Army, for its final descent to landing.

The first X-38, known as Vehicle 131, arrived at Dryden on 4 June 1997 and made its maiden flight in March 1998. The second aircraft, V132, was delivered to Dryden in September 1998 and made four unpowered drop tests. Unfortunately, the X-38 program was cancelled in late 2002 before a space-rated vehicle had been assembled. Both completed airframes are in storage at the NASA Johnson Space Center in Houston.

Air Force Research Laboratory

X-39

First Flight:	Pending	**Sponsors:**	USAF
Last Flight:	Not Applicable	**Fastest Flight:**	Not Applicable
Total Flights:	Not Applicable	**Highest Flight:**	Not Applicable

Speculative artist concept of a possible unmanned aerial vehicle that could be similar to the X-39.
(U.S. Air Force via the Dennis R. Jenkins Collection)

The X-39 designator was apparently reserved for use by the Air Force Research Laboratory for subscale unmanned demonstrators originally planned under the Future Aircraft Technology Enhancements (FATE) program. FATE was intended to develop revolutionary technologies that would become the foundation for next generation of combat aircraft. Examples of FATE technologies included affordable low-observable data systems, active aeroelastic wing, robust composite sandwich structures, advanced compact inlets, photonic vehicle management systems, self-adaptive flight controls, and electric flight control actuators.

A subset of the Fixed Wing Vehicle (FWV) program, FATE was divided into three primary phases: Phase I was to define a set of aircraft technologies for both inhabited and uninhabited aircraft. Phase II was to develop preliminary vehicle design concepts, a demonstrator system, and demonstration plans. Phase III would develop, build, and flight-test a demonstrator vehicle. It is known that at least Boeing Seattle and Boeing Phantom Works participated in the program. Phase I was apparently used as a jump start for the Unmanned Combat Air Vehicle (UCAV) programs, and the rest of FATE was seemingly cancelled before being started.

X-40A

The Boeing Company

First Flight:	11 August 1998	**Sponsors:**	USAF, NASA
Last Flight:	18 May 2001	**Fastest Flight:**	300 mph (approx)
Total Flights:	8	**Highest Flight:**	15,000 feet (approx)

The X-40A landing after Free Flight 4A on 5 May 2001. (NASA photo EC01-0145-12 by Tom Tschida)

The X-40A was an 80-percent scale version of a proposed Space Maneuver Vehicle (SMV) that has become the X-37. The SMV was designed to deliver small satellites, perform on-orbit reconnaissance, and other duties. The X-40A completed a successful autonomous approach and landing on its first flight test on 11 August 1998 after being dropped from an Army UH-60 Black Hawk helicopter at an altitude of 9,000 feet over the White Sands Missile Range. The vehicle used an integrated INS/GPS to touch down on a hard surface runway.

After its single test flight, the Air Force gave the X-40A to NASA for use as a prototype of the X-37 vehicle, and the X-40A arrived at the Dryden Flight Research Center on 26 May 2000. In a concurrent test program to support the low-speed atmospheric flight dynamics of the X-37 design, the X-40A successfully completed its flight test program with seven successful flights at Edwards. During the series of flights, the unmanned X-40A was released from a CH-47 Chinook helicopter at 15,000 feet, and it autonomously acquired the runway and landed in a mode similar to a conventional aircraft. The X-40A demonstrated the guidance, navigation & control algorithms, software, calculated air data system, integrated GPS/INS, and aerodynamic performance of the basic X-37, and also used its mobile flight operations control center. The X-40A is currently in storage at the Boeing facility in Seal Beach, California.

Unknown

X-41

First Flight:	Unknown	**Sponsors:**	USAF
Last Flight:	Not Applicable	**Fastest Flight:**	Not Applicable
Total Flights:	Not Applicable	**Highest Flight:**	Not Applicable

No Illustration
Available

No photographs or artist concepts have been released of the X-41 to date.

The X-41 Common Aero Vehicle (CAV) involves an experimental maneuverable reentry vehicle carrying a variety of payloads through a suborbital trajectory, and reentering and dispersing the payload in the atmosphere.

The CAV program was originally slated for a flight demonstration during 2003, but the current intentions are unknown. It is likely that the program has been cancelled. The CAV was to provide both an expendable and future reusable Military Space Plane (MSP) system architecture with the ability to deploy multiple payload types from and through space to a terrestrial target. The program was to demonstrate a high terminal accuracy, extended cross-range, and high maneuverability in a low-cost expendable or single use package.

X-42

Unknown

First Flight:	Unknown	**Sponsors:**	USAF
Last Flight:	Not Applicable	**Fastest Flight:**	Not Applicable
Total Flights:	Not Applicable	**Highest Flight:**	Not Applicable

No Illustration
Available

No photographs or artist concepts have been released of the X-42 to date.

The X-42 Pop-Up Upper Stage is an experimental expendable liquid-fueled upper stage designed to boost 2,000–4,000-pound payloads into orbit. Pop-Up Upper Stages can expand the utility of advanced military spacecraft, allowing for wider ranges of payload deployment. This project reportedly includes technologies that will improve pop-up upper stage technologies and/or stages themselves. The X-42 will demonstrate individual orbit transfer propulsion capabilities that significantly enhance low-cost, high-performance access to space via revolutionary propulsion techniques with improved designs, combustion and mixing technologies, and material advancements. It will also develop and demonstrate chemical propulsion systems for military, civil, and commercial orbit transfer applications. Future orbit transfer systems will require advanced materials, low-cost power processing developments, and increased thruster efficiency.

The current status of this program is unknown, and it is possible that it has been cancelled.

Microcraft, Inc.

X-43

First Flight: 2 June 2001

Last Flight: Not Applicable

Total Flights: Not Applicable

Sponsors: NASA

Fastest Flight: Not Applicable

Highest Flight: Not Applicable

The first X-43A undergoes final checkout prior to its ill-fated flight. Shortly after launch from the NB-52B the Pegasus launch vehicle veered out of control and was destroyed by the Range Safety Officer. (NASA photo by Tom Tschida)

The X-43A Hyper-X program seeks to overcome one of the greatest aeronautical research challenges—air-breathing hypersonic flight. The X-43A vehicles were intended fly at speeds of Mach 7 and 10, and the goal of the Hyper-X program is to validate key propulsion and related technologies for air-breathing hypersonic aircraft. The vehicles were not designed to be recovered, and all data will be telemetered to the ground during the flight.

The first X-43A and its modified Pegasus booster were carried aloft by the NASA NB-52B carrier aircraft from Dryden Flight Research Center on 2 June 2001 for the first of three high-speed free flight attempts. About an hour and 15 minutes later the Pegasus booster was released from the NB-52B to accelerate the X-43A to its intended speed of Mach 7. However, the combined Pegasus and X-43A "stack" lost control about eight seconds after Pegasus ignition; the mission was terminated by the Range Safety Officer, and the Pegasus and X-43A fell into the Pacific Ocean in a cleared Navy range area. The second X-43A flight is currently scheduled for late 2003 after certain hardware and procedural modifications are made to the remaining Hyper-X vehicles and their Pegasus boosters. A follow-on X-43C program is also under discussion using larger vehicles and higher speeds.

The X-43B (Reusable Combined Cycle Flight Demonstrator Project) is proposed to demonstrate/validate the selected propulsion system for a rocket-based combined cycle (RBCC), turbine-based combined cycle (TBCC), or a combination RBCC/TBCC propulsion system in the 0.7–7.0 Mach range.

The X-43C Project is a joint effort between NASA and the United States Air Force (USAF), using propulsion technology developed in the Air Force HyTech Program. The project will demonstrate powered flight of a hypersonic aircraft accelerating from Mach 5 to Mach 7, using an airframe-integrated, fuel-cooled, dual-mode scramjet propulsion system with hydrocarbon fuel. The purpose of this research is to validate the technology, computational methods, and experimental techniques required to design and predict performance of future air-breathing operational vehicles for space access.

X-44 Lockheed Martin Corporation

First Flight:	Pending	**Sponsors:**	USAF, NASA
Last Flight:	Not Applicable	**Fastest Flight:**	Not Applicable
Total Flights:	Not Applicable	**Highest Flight:**	Not Applicable

A speculative artist concept of the Lockheed Martin X-44 tailless research aircraft. (Image retouching by Brian Duke)

The X-44 designation is reportedly reserved for a possible full-scale USAF/NASA manned tailless flight control demonstrator. The X-44 has been referred to as the MANTA, or Multi-Axis No-Tail Aircraft.

The plan is to convert an early prototype Lockheed Martin F-22 Raptor with a large delta wing (similar to that proposed for the FB-22) and advanced thrust vectoring nozzles for flight control. Thrust vectoring—the ability to turn the jet exhaust—allows an aircraft to create forces with its engines similar to the forces created by aerodynamic surfaces such as flaps, rudders, and stabilators. The result would be a structurally simple, light airframe, with increased fuel volume and better "stealth" characteristics since there would be no movable aerodynamic control surfaces. An X-44 feasibility study is in progress, with a team including AFRL, NASA, Lockheed Martin, and Pratt & Whitney. The X-44 is unlikely to fly before 2007, although the F-22 program will retire the first and second flying prototypes long before then. The X-44 technology, combined with fluidic nozzles and supersonic-cruise aerodynamics, could lead to a generation of high-performance, very stealthy aircraft, with exceptionally high aerodynamic efficiency.

The Boeing Company

X-45

First Flight:	22 May 2002	**Sponsors:**	DARPA, USAF, Boeing
Last Flight:	Not Applicable	**Fastest Flight:**	Unknown
Total Flights:	On-going	**Highest Flight:**	Unknown

The first X-45A UCAV (Unmanned Combat Air Vehicle) at the NASA Dryden Flight Research Center.
(NASA photo ED02-0295-05)

The X-45 was developed by the Boeing (former McDonnell Douglas) Phantom Works in St. Louis, Missouri. The X-45 unmanned combat air vehicle (UCAV) is a tailless, 27-foot-long, jet-powered aircraft with a 34-foot wingspan. The vehicle incorporates a thrust vectoring system for yaw control, thus eliminating the need for vertical stabilizers, reducing the drag and radar cross-section.

The UCAV System Demonstration Program is a joint DARPA/USAF/Boeing effort to demonstrate the technical feasibility for a UCAV system to conduct various strike missions within the emerging global command and control architecture. The demonstrations will provide the information necessary to enable decision-makers to determine whether it is technically and fiscally prudent to continue development of a production UCAV. Two X-45A aircraft completed 16 flights during Phase I testing which ended in February 2003.

Initial plans for an X-45B version were apparently cancelled in mid-2003, with the program moving directly to a more capable X-45C due to a change in mission requirements.

X-46

The Boeing Company

First Flight:	Pending	**Sponsors:**	DARPA, USN, Boeing
Last Flight:	Not Applicable	**Fastest Flight:**	Not Applicable
Total Flights:	Not Applicable	**Highest Flight:**	Not Applicable

An artist's concept of the UCAV-N landing on an aircraft carrier.
(Boeing via Erik Simonsen)

On 30 June 2000 DARPA and the U.S. Navy awarded two contracts for the first phase of the Naval Unmanned Combat Air Vehicle (UCAV-N) Advanced Technology Program (ATP). Boeing and Northrop Grumman will each receive $2 million for the initial 15-month trade study, analyses, and preliminary design phase.

The goal of the joint DARPA/Navy project is to demonstrate the technical feasibility for a Naval UCAV system to effectively and affordably conduct sea-based suppression of enemy air defenses, strike, and surveillance missions. At the conclusion of the15-month preliminary design phase, DoD will decide whether to proceed with the second phase. DoD would select one or both contractors for the second phase to complete the development and demonstration of critical UCAV-N system technologies. The UCAV-N program takes advantage of the work carried out under the DARPA/USAF UCAV program. However, the naval program adds surveillance to the mission set, and will include a significant focus on issues of naval shipboard integration. Initially, the program will emphasize a vehicle that can be launched from existing aircraft carriers using the standard catapult, and recovered using the existing arresting system. Other techniques may be investigated later during the program.

Northrop-Grumman

X-47

First Flight:	24 February 2003	**Sponsors:**	DARPA, USN, Northrop
Last Flight:	Not Applicable	**Fastest Flight:**	Not Applicable
Total Flights:	Ongoing	**Highest Flight:**	Not Applicable

The overall shape of the X-47A is very reminiscent of the "hopeless diamond" originally conceived during the development of the F-117 stealth fighter. Note the complete lack of vertical control surfaces. (Northrop Grumman)

At the same time that Boeing was awarded the contract for their UCAV-N demonstrator, Northrop Grumman was awarded a similar contract for a different design. The initial Pegasus carries the designation X-47A, and a refined UCAV-N is expected to be designated the X-47B. Designed with stealth features and shaped like a kite, Pegasus is constructed largely with composite materials. One of the first tasks of the Pegasus flight program will be to demonstrate acceptable aerodynamic flying qualities suitable for operations from an aircraft carrier.

Northrop Grumman is performing trade studies, analysis and preliminary design for a UCAV-N under a $2 million contract with DARPA and the U.S. Navy. The goal of the joint DARPA/Navy project is to demonstrate the technical feasibility for a UCAV system to effectively and affordably conduct sea-based surveillance, suppression of enemy air defenses, and strike missions within the emerging global command and control architecture.

The X-47A made its first flight on 24 February 2003 at NAS China Lake, California.

X-48

The Boeing Company

First Flight:	Pending	**Sponsors:**	Boeing, NASA
Last Flight:	Not Applicable	**Fastest Flight:**	Not Applicable
Total Flights:	Not Applicable	**Highest Flight:**	Not Applicable

An artist's concept of a full-size Blended Wing Body aircraft in the refueling role.
(Boeing via Erik Simonsen)

The Boeing Phantom Works is currently developing the Blended Wing Body (BWB) aircraft concept in cooperation with the NASA Langley Research Center. In a continuing effort to study the flight characteristics of the BWB design, a small remote controlled model has been successfully flown. The next step is to fly the 35-foot long X-48 currently being built at Langley. Test flights are scheduled to begin in 2004.

The BWB concept reportedly offers greater structural, aerodynamic and operating efficiencies than today's more conventional tube-and-wing designs. Its modular design also allows for center body growth while maintaining common wings. These features translate into greater range, fuel economy, reliability and life cycle savings, as well as lower manufacturing costs. They also allow for a wide variety of potential military and commercial applications.

Unassigned

X-49

First Flight:

Sponsors:

Last Flight:

Fastest Flight:

Total Flights:

Highest Flight:

No Illustration Available

No photographs or artist concepts of the X-49 have been released.

As of early 2003 the X-49 designator had apparently been skipped because DARPA requested the X-50 designation for the Dragonfly Canard Rotor/Wing demonstrator. DARPA reportedly wanted the number 50 under the theory that the CRW would be the first true 50/50 marriage of helicopters and high-speed fixed wing aircraft.

It is likely that the X-49 designation will be assigned when the next X designator is requested.

X-50

The Boeing Company

First Flight:	Pending	**Sponsors:**	DARPA, Boeing
Last Flight:	Not Applicable	**Fastest Flight:**	Not Applicable
Total Flights:	Not Applicable	**Highest Flight:**	Not Applicable

The Boeing Dragonfly demonstrator vehicle showing its centrally mounted rotary wing, its movable forward canards, and its fixed horizontal stabilizer. (Boeing via Erik Simonsen)

In June 1998 a $24 million agreement between DARPA and The Boeing Company funded a 37 month effort by the Boeing Phantom Works to design, build, and fly two technology demonstrators to assess and validate the X-50 Dragonfly Canard Rotor/Wing (CRW) advanced rotorcraft. Each contributed $12 million toward the program.

The unmanned X-50A CRW is 17.7 feet long, 6.5 feet high, and the rotor blades have a diameter of 12 feet. Powered by a conventional turbofan engine, the X-50A will use diverter valves to direct thrust to the rotor blade tips (for helicopter mode), or aft to the jet nozzle (for fixed wing mode). Dual bleed thrust will be used during transition. By directing thrust through the rotor tips, the CRW concept eliminates the need for a heavy and complex mechanical drive train, transmission and anti-torque system.

Aviation enthusiasts may have noticed that the X-50 designation was not the next in line. But Steve Bass, Boeing's X-50 program manager, confirms Boeing got the number out of sequence by special request. The X-50 designation is so fitting for the CRW concept—50 percent helicopter and 50 percent airplane.

LIFTING BODIES

First Flight:	16 August 1963 (M2-F1)	**Sponsors:**	NASA
Last Flight:	17 July 1970 (HL-10)	**Fastest Flight:**	Mach 1.86 (HL-10)
Total Flights:	43 (M2) / 37 (HL-10)	**Highest Flight:**	90,303 feet (HL-10)

The three lifting bodies tested during the 1960s: The Air Force X-24 (described separately) is at left, the M2-F3 is in the center, and the HL-10 is at right. All proved to be remarkably capable machines, especially given the limited budget used for their development.

The lifting body program involved several separate vehicles—the X-23s, X-24, M2, and HL-10—that provided data on wingless lifting bodies from orbital reentry velocities to approach and landing speeds. The X-23 and X-24 programs are discussed earlier in this publication.

The piloted lifting body program began in September 1962 when R. Dale Reed, at the NASA Flight Research Center, began work on the M2-F1. This plywood vehicle was towed behind various trucks and cars to get airborne, and proved the basic concept. NASA then awarded a contract to Northrop to build a metal version called the M2-F2, powered by a Reaction Motors XLR11 rocket engine left over from the X-15 program. After a serious crash on 10 May 1967 the airframe was rebuilt as the M2-F3 with a central vertical stabilizer that largely cured an earlier stability problem.

The HL-10 was a totally different shape, but shared many common systems with the M2-F2/3 and was also powered by an XLR11. Its first flight was on 22 December 1966, and the HL-10 would ultimately become the fastest and highest flying of the manned lifting bodies.

D-558 Douglas Aircraft Company

First Flight:	14 April 1947 (-I)	**Sponsors:**	USN, NACA
Last Flight:	12 December 1956 (-II)	**Fastest Flight:**	650.8 mph / 1,291 mph
Total Flights:	228 (-I) / 161 (-II)	**Highest Flight:**	40,000+ feet / 83,235 feet

The D-558-I used straight wings and a single turbojet engine—the D-558-II used swept wings and the same Reaction Motors XLR11 that powered the X-1 (and many others). This October 1949 photo shows the Skystreak in its later white paint scheme with an early NACA shield on the vertical stabilizer. (NASA photo E49-090)

Usually overlooked when X-vehicles are discussed, the two Navy-sponsored Douglas D-558 designs did not use the Air Force "X" designation series, but nevertheless played an important role in advancing aeronautics during the late 1940s and early 1950s. In the public's mind, much of the research performed by the D-558-I Skystreaks was quickly overshadowed by Chuck Yeager and the X-1. Regardless, the Skystreak performed an important role in aeronautical research by flying for extended periods of time at transonic speeds, complementing the X-1 that flew for limited periods at supersonic speeds. The later D-558-IIs would follow the X-1's lead and use rocket propulsion.

The three D-558-I Skystreaks were turbojet-powered aircraft that took off from the ground under their own power. The first aircraft is on display at the Naval Aviation Museum in Pensacola, Florida. The second D-558-I crashed on 3 May 1948, killing NACA pilot Howard C. Lilly. The third Skystreak is owned by the Carolinas Historical Aviation Museum located at the Charlotte International Airport in North Carolina.

The rocket-powered air-launched D-558-II Skyrocket became the first aircraft to exceed Mach 2. The first D-558-II is on display at the Planes of Fame Museum in Chino, California. The number two Skyrocket, the aircraft used by Scott Crossfield to first break Mach 2, is on display at the National Air and Space Museum in Washington DC. The last D-558-II is displayed on a pedestal at Antelope Valley College, Lancaster, California.

Test pilot A. Scott Crossfield used one of the D-558-IIs to become the first person to exceed twice the speed of sound—barely—he managed Mach 2.005 on 20 November 1953 after being dropped from a Boeing P2B-1S (the Navy designation for the B-29), similar to the one in the background. (NASA photo E-2499)

The NACA hangar at Edwards in 1953. The three D-558-IIs are against the left wall, with one of the D-558-Is facing the camera. The wing of the YF-84A is in the foreground, with an early B-47 looming over the smaller research aircraft. (NASA photo E-959)